D1613760

4/11

DEMCO

Kelsey's **K** Book

WRITTEN BY **J. L. MAZZEO**
ILLUSTRATED BY **HELEN ROSS REVUTSKY**

•••• dingles & company New Jersey

©2007 by Judith Mazzeo Zocchi

First Printing

Published By dingles&company
P.O. Box 508
Sea Girt, New Jersey 08750

LIBRARY OF CONGRESS CATALOG CARD NUMBER
2005907203

ISBN
ISBN-13: 978 1-59646-476-6
ISBN-10: 1-59646-476-3

Printed in the United States of America

My Letter Library series is based on the original concept of Judy Mazzeo Zocchi.

ART DIRECTION
Barbie Lambert & Rizco Design

DESIGN
Rizco Design

EDITED BY
Andrea Curley

PROJECT MANAGER
Lisa Aldorasi

EDUCATIONAL CONSULTANT
Maura Ruane McKenna

PRE-PRESS BY
Pixel Graphics

EXPLORE THE LETTERS OF THE ALPHABET WITH MY LETTER LIBRARY*

Aimee's **A** Book
Bebe's **B** Book
Cassie's **C** Book
Delia's **D** Book
Emma's **E** Book
Faye's **F** Book
George's **G** Book
Henry's **H** Book
Izzy's **I** Book
Jade's **J** Book
Kelsey's **K** Book
Logan's **L** Book
Mia's **M** Book
Nate's **N** Book
Owen's **O** Book
Peter's **P** Book
Quinn's **Q** Book
Rosie's **R** Book
Sofie's **S** Book
Tad's **T** Book
Uri's **U** Book
Vera's **V** Book
Will's **W** Book
Xavia's **X** Book
Yola's **Y** Book
Zach's **Z** Book

* All titles also available in bilingual English/Spanish versions.

WEBSITE
www.dingles.com

E-MAIL
info@dingles.com

My **Letter** Library

K k

My Letter Library leads young children through the alphabet one letter at a time. By focusing on an individual letter in each book, the series allows youngsters to identify and absorb the concept of each letter thoroughly before being introduced to the next. In addition, it invites them to look around and discover where objects beginning with the specific letter appear in their own world.

Kk

A a   B b   C c   D d   E e   F f   G g

H h   I i   J j   **K k**   L l   M m   N n

O o   P p   Q q   R r   S s   T t   U u

V v   W w   X x   Y y   Z z

K is for Kelsey.

Kelsey is a kind koala.

Near the top of Kelsey's tree
you will find a **k**iwi
she bought at the market,

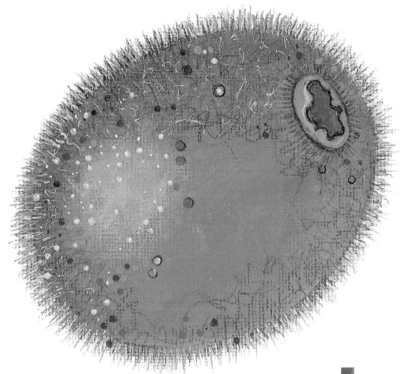

Kk

a **k**ey to a castle door,

Kk

and a **k**ookaburra

waiting for the rain to stop.

Kk

On the ground
by Kelsey's tree
you will find a **k**itten,

K k

a **k**ite for flying,

K k

and a **k**ing who is

needed in his kingdom.

K k

Behind Kelsey's tree

you will see a **k**night

in shining armor,

K k

a **k**angaroo

who is ready for school,

K k

and a **k**atydid

who rubs his wings

together to make music.

K k

Things that begin with
the letter **K** are all around.

KIWI

KEY

KOOKABURRA

KITTEN

KITE

KING

KNIGHT

KANGAROO

KATYDID

Where around Kelsey's tree
can they be found?

Have a **"K"** Day!

Read "K" stories all day long.
Read books about kittens, kites, koalas, kiwis, and other **K** words. Then have the child pick out all of the words and pictures starting with the letter **K**.

Make a "K" Craft: Colorful Kite
Cut a 10-x-13-inch sheet of paper into the shape of a diamond.

Next, have the child use watercolor or tempera paint to decorate the diamond shape. He or she can simply swirl colors on the diamond or paint pictures of objects that begin with the letter **K**.

Make a tail by cutting a strip of paper 2 inches wide by 12 inches long and gluing or stapling one end of it to the bottom of the kite.

Using a 3-x-3-inch piece of paper, cut out a bow. (It should look like two triangles connected at the top points.)

Have the child glue or staple the bow to the bottom of the tail.

Hang the Colorful Kite on a window and imagine it flying through the sky!

Make a "K" Snack: Kangaroo Pouches
- Cut a pita pocket bread in half.
- Have a selection of foods that the child enjoys to eat, such as peanut butter, cream cheese, egg salad, tuna salad, or cold cuts.
- Allow your child to stuff the pita and eat the Kangaroo Pouch!

For additional **"K"** Day ideas and a reading list, go to www.dingles.com.

About **Letters**

Use the My Letter Library series to teach a child to identify letters and recognize the sounds they make by hearing them used and repeated in each story.

Ask:
- What letter is this book about?
- Can you name all of the **K** pictures on each page?
- Which **K** picture is your favorite? Why?
- Can you find all of the words in this book that begin with the letter **K**?

ENVIRONMENT
Discuss objects that begin with the letter **K** in the child's immediate surroundings and environment.

Use these questions to further the conversation:
- Do you have a kite? If so, where do you fly it?
- Do you have a kitten? If so, what is his or her name?
- Do you have a favorite food that begins with the letter **K**? What is it?

- Have you every seen a kangaroo? If so, where?

OBSERVATIONS
The My Letter Library series can be used to enhance the child's imagination. Encourage the child to look around and tell you what he or she sees.

Ask:
- Do you ever pretend to live in a castle? If so, who do you pretend to be?
- Who would you like to live with in your pretend castle?
- Have you ever dressed up like a knight? If so, was it fun?
- What is your favorite **K** object at home? Why?

TRY SOMETHING NEW...
Find ways to be kind to your family and neighbors. For instance, you could take out the trash for an elderly or disabled neighbor, do extra chores around the house, or make time to play with a younger sibling or friend!

J. L. MAZZEO grew up in Middletown, New Jersey, as part of a close-knit Italian American family. She currently resides in Monmouth County, New Jersey, and still remains close to family members in heart and home.

HELEN ROSS REVUTSKY was born in St. Petersburg, Russia, where she received a degree in stage artistry/design. She worked as the directing artist in Kiev's famous Governmental Puppet Theatre. Her first book, *I Can Read the Alphabet,* was published in Moscow in 1998. Helen now lives in London, where she has illustrated several children's books.